GOLF

Stories
Beliefs
and
Rarities

By Dave Sommerhauser

Illustrated By Art Heyne

Introduction:

This book is a collection of stories, quips, quotes, jokes, beliefs and more, from caddies, pros, movie stars and the average golfer who wanted to get his two cents worth in. By reading this book you will gain some knowledge of golf, the tournaments and the people who play in them. Who knows, you may even have a laugh or two. This book will not help you with your golf game. For that you need commitment and practice.

ISBN: 0-7392-0127-1
Library of Congress Catalog Card Number: 99-93638

Printed in the USA by

3212 East Highway 30 • Kearney, NE 68847 • 1-800-650-7888

In 1955 Life Magazine paid Ben Hogan $20,000 for his secret of how he eliminated his hook.

Why do many pros stare at their coin before they put it down to mark their ball on the green? Most of the time it is superstition. Many pros have quirks in marking a ball on the green with a coin in a certain manner. Some always place the coin heads up with the face looking at the hole. Others are making sure that they are using their lucky coin. If they have to move their mark for another player, many will place it wrong side up to remind themselves to move it back to the original spot before they putt. We have all played with people who have a certain way to place their coin. Like putting it four inches in front of the spot where the ball rest.

In 1892 Shinnecock Hills Golf Club built the first clubhouse in the United States. Shinnecock Hills was also the first club to have a waiting list.

Many people think that a golf shot with a draw travels farther because it has top-spin. In fact, it has no top-spin at all. It simply has less backspin.

Chi Chi Rodriquez was telling about his life as a boy and said, "We where so poor that when I was a boy the biggest present I got was a marble.

Gene Sarazen was baptized Eugene Saraceni but changed his name when he saw it in the paper after he had won a local golf tournament. "I had to," he said. "My old name was fine for a violin player but lousy for a golfer."

Early in their careers Sam Snead and Johnny Bulla became friends. The tour would start each year in California and the two of them drove out there together to save on expenses. In a practice that was not uncommon at the time, Sam suggested that whatever money they won that year they would split the winnings. Bulla thought about it and decided he would take his chances on his own game. Bad choice. Snead won five tournaments that year and had three seconds and five thirds. He had twenty-three top ten finishes in all and came in second on the money list. It would be two years before Bulla got his first win. In a way it's a good thing that they never pooled their winnings. With all the research I have done on Sam Snead, I am certain that if they had it would have been Sam's last year on tour. Giving away half of his winnings would have killed him.

Why is the stretch between the eleventh and thirteenth holes at Augusta National called "Amen Corner?" The origin of the term "Amen Corner," is unknown but many pros believe that if you can negotiate these three holes in par a prayer is in order. Over the years these three holes have had a long history in deciding the outcome of the Masters.

A young pro once told Ben Hogan he was having trouble with 30 and 40 foot putts and asked if he could give him some advice. Hogan didn't even pause to think. He just said "ya, hit the ball closer to the hole."

The first person to make one million dollars on the PGA tour was Arnold Palmer.

In 1911 Johnny McDermott became the first American golfer to win the U.S. Open Championship and was able to retain the title the following year.

In 1922 Walter Hagen became the first golf professional to start a golf equipment company.

If you think your a bad putter, you may want to compare your stats with these of the pros. Touring pros make only 55% of their six-foot putts. Only 33% of their ten-foot putts. One in six of their fifteen-foot putts and only 10% of their twenty-five foot putts. Where we as average golfers differ from the pros, is that the pros rarely three putt.

Chi Chi Rodriquez got his first professional victory at the 1963 Denver Open. His first place check was worth $5,300. He took the money and bought his mom a modest home in Puerto Rico.

The length of the average drive on tour in 1968 was 258 yards. In 1995 it was 263 yards. That's an improvement of only five yards in 27 years.

Walter Hagen and Joe Kirkwood, two of the biggest names in golf in 1923 were the first to use and advertise the wooden golf tee.

Golf is a lot of walking broken up by disappointments and bad arithmetic.

People who have shot 60 in a PGA event:

~ ~ ~ ~ ~ ~

Al Brosch	1951
Bill Nary	1952
Ted Kroll	1954
Tommy Bolt	1954
Mike Souchak	1955
Sam Sneed	1957
David Frost	1990
Davis Love III	1994
Steve Lowery	1997

~ ~ ~ ~ ~ ~

In the 1986 Masters, Seve Ballesteros four putted the 16th green. When he was asked how he did that he said, "I miss the putt. I miss the putt. I miss the putt. I make."

The PGA outlawed the practice of paying appearance money to top pros because several agencies gained to much power by having many of the big-name players as clients. Such an agency could make or break a tournament just by the number of big names that they could promise or withhold. The PGA prohibited this practice in order to help tournament committees, television and the golf fans.

The first Japanese golfer to win a PGA tour event was Isao Aoki, when he won the 1983 Hawaiian Open.

Why was croquet-style putting outlawed?
Rule 16-1e prohibits standing astride or on the line of a putt. Croquet-style putting enjoyed a brief period of popularity when Sam Sneed used it to cure his "yips". The croquet-style was never a traditional golf stroke and never considered a fair stroke. Additionally, a player would gain a distinct advantage by being able to sight directly down the line of a putt as compared to a traditional manner of putting. Rule 16-1e was put into effect to preserve the traditional and inherent fairness of the game.

"**P**rayer never seems to work for me on the golf course. I think this has something to do with my being a terrible putter." (Billy Graham)

"**P**lease stop checking your watch all the time, it's distracting my game." The golfer said to his caddie after hitting his eight shot from the woods. The caddie replied. "This isn't a watch, sir, It's a compass."

If you think you felt bad the last time you took an eight or a nine on a hole, how do you think these professional golfers felt when they turned in these scores?

◇ ◇ ◇ ◇

12 For Arnold Palmer in the 1961 L. A. Open.

13 For Tommy Nakajima in the 1978 Masters.

14 For Greg Norman in the 1982 Martini International.

16 For Ian Woosnam at the 1986 French Open.

18 For John Daly at the 1998 Bay Hill Invitational.

19 For Ray Ainsley in the 1938 U. S. Open.

21 For Philippe Porquier at the 1978 French Open.

<u>Last but not least</u>
"Mr. self-control"
Tommy Bolt
took 23 strokes
to hole out on
a hole at the 1927
Shawnee Open.

IF I SINK THIS IT WILL GIVE ME A COOL 23

Raymond Floyd was the oldest player ever to compete in the Ryder Cup and sank the winning putt that year for the United States at the Belfry. The year was 1993 and Floyd was 53 years old at the time.

The less skilled the player, the more likely he is to share his ideas about how to improve your golf swing.

Here's a tip for you. Let the Yellow Pages do the swinging for you. Try swinging your left arm while holding a phone book. It will build the muscles of your forearm, shoulder and wrist to give you a little more power in your left side. In some cities I've visited you may want to use some other type of weight. Have you seen the size of some of those phone books?

Steel shafts where approved by the United States Golf Association for tournament play in 1923. The Royal and Ancient Golf Club did not approve them until 1930.

In 1978 Nancy Lopez won five tournaments in a row and nine tournaments in all. Not bad for her first season.

Bobby Jones played as an amateur his entire career.

In 1975, 21 year old Joe Flynn set a record for the lowest score for eighteen holes while throwing the ball. His score was 82, on the Port Royal Course in Bermuda. This has to be a short course.

Top ten consecutive years with a win.

Jack Nicklaus 17

Billy Casper 16

Lee Trevino 14

Sam Sneed 11

Harry Cooper 11

Leo Diegel 11

Arnold Palmer 10

Lloyd Mangrum 9

Ben Hogan 9

Walter Hagen 9

Back in the 30s, entering the U.S. Open wasn't anything like it is today and nowhere near as strict. In fact, just a few months before the 1935 U.S. Open, the USGA received a letter that simply said, "Enter me, Jim." Jimmy Demaret thought that would be good enough but he didn't want to take any chances that they may not receive it in time. He sent it "airmail" from a post office eleven blocks from the USGA office.

When Jack Fleck won the 1955 U.S. Open at San Francisco's Olympic Club it was like the Rocky movie. A pro from a municipal golf course in Davenport, Iowa beating the likes of Ben Hogan, Sam Snead, and Cary Middlecoff. In fact when Hogan finished 72 holes as the leader of the Championship, he signed his score card and tossed the ball to Joe Dey, the executive director of the USGA. "Here, Joe," Hogan said. "This is for Golf House." Then he waited. There was only one person who could tie him and that was Fleck. He would have to birdie two of the last four holes to do it. Someone said that a reporter told Hogan what Fleck would have to do and Hogan said, "well good luck to him," and headed for the shower. Fleck came to the final hole needing a birdie to tie Hogan. His tee shot went into the left rough but his approach shot left him with a ten foot putt. He wasted no time and drained the putt, sending the Championship into an 18 hole playoff the next day, which Jack Fleck won.

Granted his career isn't what it once was, but Greg Norman was the first tour player to surpass the ten million dollar mark in winnings.

To date, nobody has ever shot four rounds in the 60's at the Masters.

Scotland has the earliest written evidence of the existence of golf. In 1457 King James II proclaimed that the game of golf was to be banned. The Kings reason was that golf was taking up valuable time that should have been spent practicing archery, swordsmanship and other defensive skills.

The forerunner of the U.S. Open took place in 1894. Willie Dunn won the matchplay event. A year later the first official U.S. Open took place at Newport, Rhode Island on October 4, 1895.

Patent number 08/723,608 was issued to the Wilson Company for golf's first titanium core golf ball in 1997.

Why is it that most beginners in golf start out slicing instead of hooking? There are two main reasons for this pattern: grip and swing plane. Most people who grip a golf club for the first time hold it so that the left hand is turned to the right, a very natural way to hold a club and the preferred method for gripping a baseball bat. However, in golf the wrist turn or pronate and do not break as in baseball. This incorrect grip leaves the face of the club open, and the ball flies off with sidespin. The beginner also has a tendency to hit the ball from the outside, which produces a sidespin as well. The inside-out swing plane seems counterproductive to the raw beginner who is slicing the ball to the right anyway.

In 1963, Bob Charles became the first lefty to win on tour when he won the British Open.

Tom Watson won five British Opens, each on a different course.

Kathy Whitworth, LPGA Hall of Famer has 88 professional victories, the most of any golfer, male or female.

A tour pro will change balls every few holes because golf balls tend to get out of round after being hit several times. He is not that concerned about shot making as much as putting because an out of round ball will not roll in a true manner. I wonder how many balls get switched by the caddy when the pro marks and flips it to him? A lot can go on inside of a towel.

The evolution of the PGA purse in 5 year segments.

1950 $459,950
1955 $782,010
1960 $1,335,242
1965 $2,848,515
1970 $6,751,523
1975 $7,895,450
1980 $13,371,786
1985 $25,290,526
1990 $46,251,831
1995 $62,250,000

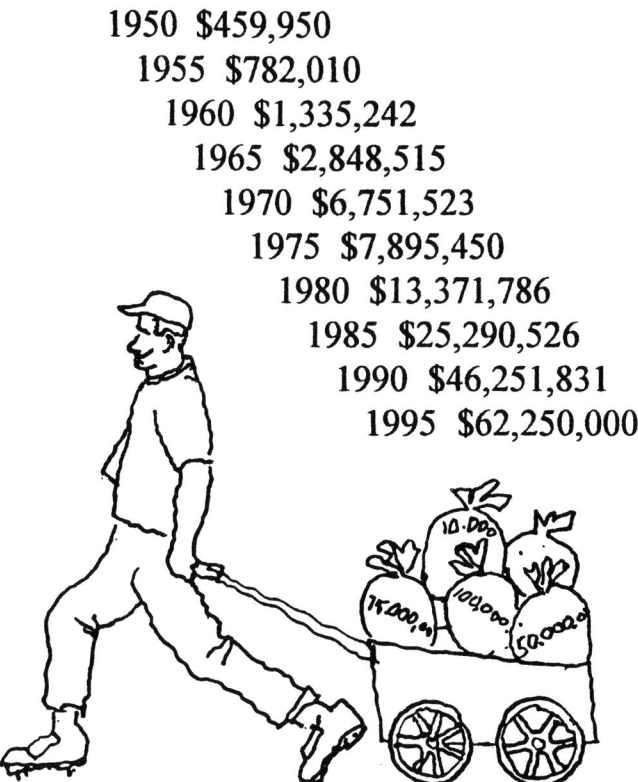

In 1945-1946 there were 73 pro tour events in the United States. Ben Hogan and Byron Nelson won 57.5% of them.

A typical 5-iron in 1980 had 32 degrees loft. A typical 5-iron in 1997 has 27 degrees of loft. Did you really think it was your practicing that gave you the extra yardage?

The follow-through is the part of the swing that takes place after the ball has been hit but before the club has been thrown.

There have been 29 U.S. Opens that have ended in a playoff.

The youngest person ever to get a hole in one is Matthew Stewart of Washington Indiana. On August 3rd 1998, at the age of 5 years and 3 months aced the 86 yard par 3 number 7 at the Fox Ridge Country Club using his driver.

In 1953 Ben Hogan won 3 of the 4 majors. He did not play in the fourth, the PGA Championship.

Why is the PGA Tour considered one of the most difficult major league sports to enter? To qualify for a spot on the PGA golfers must play well over a period of elimination rounds against the best players in the world. The players on tour who finish between 1 and 125 on the annual money list are exempt from qualifying. Players who finish 126 to 150 must qualify at a 108 hole tournament in December. For players seeking to break into the tour, qualifying begins in early fall with a 72 hole tournament followed by a second elimination tournament of 72 holes. The initial field of 1,750 is cut down to 155 players who join the twenty-five touring pros for the December tournament to select 50 players who will receive tour cards for the coming year. The 108 hole tournament is a pressure-packed event where one bad hole might mean not winning your tour card.

Golf Magazine was started in 1959.

No Canadian has ever won the Canadian Open.

Bets lengthen putts and shorten drives.

"My favorite shots are the practice swing and the conceded putt. The rest can never be mastered."
(Lord Robertson)

This is one of those, "suppose to be true stories." When Walter Hagen was playing in a tournament one of his approach shots landed inside of a paper bag that had blown into the bunker. When Hagen asked for a ruling he was told that he could not remove the ball without a one stroke penalty. Hagen thought about it for a moment and then calmly lit a cigarette, took a few drags, and then dropped it onto the bag, setting it on fire. Moments later he played his shot to the green and made par. Today, he would have violated at least three rules that I can think of.

Did you know that the Senior Tour was started by an idea from the man who produced "Shell's Wonderful World of Golf," Fred Raphael? He had an idea he would call "Legends of Golf" were he would have a series of matches using tour pros who were over 50. It took a few years but in 1978 NBC said they would do it but that they wanted it to be a live tournament. The first event was won by Sam Snead and Gardner Dickinson. From there it grew into the Senior Tour we have today.

Years ago you saw a lot of pros on the tour wearing a hat with the name "Amana" printed on it. The main reason for this was that Amana Refrigeration, Inc., gave a free life insurance policy to the pros who wore their hat.

Of these golf greats, who is the tallest? Lee Trevino, Gary Player, or Chi Chi Rodriguez? None of them. They all stand 5-foot-7.

An average golfer will buy a new set of irons every 5 years. That makes me below average or cheap.

Julius Boros was the oldest man to win the PGA Championship. He won the 1968 PGA Championship at the age of 48.

Have you heard the story about Sam Snead and the Pope? It seems that Sam Snead and promoter Fred Corcoran were traveling through Europe and Corcoran thought that it would be a good idea if Sam could get a visit with the Pope. He arranged the visit and when they were leaving the hotel for the Vatican he suggested that Sam bring his putter and have it blessed by the Pope. When they arrived they were met by a monsignor who told them that he to played golf and shot about 100 because of his poor putting. Sam looked at him and said, "If you're this close to the Pope and you can't putt, he ain't gonna be able to do anything for me."

In 1946, Ben Hogan's first full year back after a tour in the Army Air Corps he managed to win 13 times. To make that year even better, he came in second place 7 times. Not bad for playing in 32 tournaments. The bad news was that two of those second place finishes were in majors. The first was the Masters. Hogan hit his approach on 18 within 12 feet and needed two putts to force a playoff. Hogan missed the twelve footer and then missed the two and a half foot putt coming back. The second tragedy was the U.S. Open. Hogan had a slick 18 foot down hill putt for the win or two putts to tie. He went for the win and slid it by the hole about two feet. He missed the two foot putt coming back and he went into the history book as the second place winner.

These greens are so fast I have to hold my putter over the ball and hit it with the shadow.   (Sam Snead)

The first golf ball made in the United states was sold by A.G. Spalding in 1894.

In 1897 America's first golf magazine "Golf" hits the stands and was an immediate success.

Hagen said that no one remembers who finished second. Well they still ask me if I ever think about the putt I missed to win the 1970 British Open at St. Andrews. I tell them that sometimes it doesn't cross my mind for a full five minutes. (Doug Sanders)

The next time you see a good player stalking back and forth eyeing up a putt on the green, don't be misled by the idea that he is especially painstaking, but rather pity him for being a nervous individual who is putting off the evil moment as long as he possibly can.

Only one golfer in a thousand grips the club lightly enough. (Johnny Miller)

"My career started slowly ---
and then tapered off." (Gary McCord)

Golf World magazine was founded in 1947.

Gary Player was thinking about playing Hogan clubs at one point in his career but got a better deal from Dunlop and decided to go with them. I don't think he knew how that made Ben feel about his decision, but he would soon find out. He called Ben one night from South Africa and told him that he was having some trouble with his swing and could Ben give him some advise. "Gary, Hogan said, I'm going to be very curt with you. What kind of clubs are you playing?" "Dunlop, said Gary." "Well, Ben said, call Mr. Dunlop."

Upon receiving numerous complaints that he had made the par-3, 4th hole at Baltusrol to hard for the upcoming 1954 U.S. Open, Architect Robert Trent Jones decided to play the hole for himself and recorded a hole-in-one.

In 1961 Gary Player became the first foreign player to win the Masters.

During a thunderstorm in the second round of the 1975 Western Open, Lee Trevino, Bobby Nichols and Jerry Heard all took refuge under a large tree. Lightning struck a nearby lake and traveled through the ground to where Trevino was leaning against his golf bag. The bolt traveled up the metal shafts and pierced his left side. All three players were rushed to a nearby hospital were doctors found small exit wounds in Trevino's left shoulder. The one doctor was quoted as saying "Usually you see these marks in the morgue." Jerry Heard was able to return and tied for fourth. Bobby Nichols was burned on the head and took a few weeks off. Nichols had won 12 times in the previous 13 years on tour but after this incident, he never won another PGA Tour event.

Another story that falls in the "Hard to Believe Area." At the Mountain View Country Club in 1981, amateur Ted Barnhouse scored a hole-in-one in a most unusual fashion. On a par 3, 145 yard hole, he hit his ball to far to the right over a barbed-wire fence. The ball hit a cow which was grazing in the field in the forehead. The ball then ricocheted off the hard skull onto a sprinkler head where it then bounced and hit a lawn mower and rolled onto the green. The ball kept rolling until it hit the flagstick and fell in the hole. Now that's a hole-in-one to remember. This must be where the old saying got started. "It's not how but how many that counts,"

This would classify for the dumbest move on 1998 Europeon Tour. Ignacio Garrido was penalized four strokes for carrying an extra club in the second round of the British Masters. His caddie had forgotten and left an extra club in the bag. He finished the tournament two strokes behind the winner. It doesn't take more than 4th grade math to figure where he could have finished without the penalty strokes.

In 1930 Bobby Jones completed the original Grand Slam by winning the U.S. and British amateur and the U.S. and British Open in the same year. Since Jones was an amateur the only one that came out "smelling like a rose" financially, was professional Bobby Cruickshank who bet on Jones to complete the Slam, at 120-1 odds and pocketed $60,000. Think about it, $60,000 in 1930.

The Tournament of Champions started in 1953 and was won by Al Besselink. In 1975 it picked up a sponsor and became known as The Mony Tournament of Champions. Change came again in 1990 when it became The Infiniti Tournament of Champions.

The British Open was held at the Old Course for the first time in 1873.

1982 Who's hot and who's not?

Jerry Pate wins the Tournament Players Championship and takes Pete Dye and Commissioner Deane Beman for a swim.

Lee Trevino had his worst year in the last 15 years and finished 113th on the money list. Not to make excuses but this was a bad year also for Lee's back.

Craig Stadler puts on the classiest green jacket of all when he won the Masters Tournament by beating Dan Pohl in a playoff.

Jack Nicklaus bought the MacGregor Company.

JoAnna Carner won her way into the Hall of Fame with her 35th victory on Tour.

Bob Gilder won 3 times including the Westchester where his three wood second shot, which he thought he caught thin, finds the hole for a double-eagle.

It was a sunny Sunday morning, and Joe was beginning his pre-shot routine visualizing his upcoming shot when a voice came over the clubhouse loudspeaker. "Would the gentleman on the ladies tee please back up to the men's tee please!" Joe was still deep in his routine, seemingly impervious to the interruption. Again the announcement - "Would the man on the women's tee kindly back up to the men's tee." Joe had had enough. He shouted, "Would the announcer in the clubhouse kindly shut up and let me play my second shot."

The Byron Nelson Classic is the only PGA Tour event named after a former player.

There has been five golfers named "Sportsman of the Year." They are Arnold Palmer -- Ken Venturi -- Lee Trevino -- Jack Nicklaus and Tiger Woods.

The LPGA's Hall of Fame is considered to be one of the toughest in all of sports to get into. It has exacting criteria for admittance compared to the election format used in other sports. To be admitted to the LPGA Hall of Fame, a woman has to have thirty victories on the tour, including two different majors; or thirty-five victories with one major; or forty victories without a win in a major.

The Senior Tour is great for golf. It gives us more golf to watch and it gives the pros an extended career. When Ray Floyd was asked how he felt about turning fifty and qualifying for the Senior Tour he said, "I feel great. I went to bed and I was old and washed up. I woke up a rookie. What could be better?"

Arnold Palmer was once asked how he could have possibly made a 13 on one hole? He said "easy, I missed a 20-footer for a 12."

Up until about 65 years ago "dogleg" holes weren't around. They were designed to break the monotony of straightaway holes and afford the course architect some leeway in matching design characteristics and golf skills.

The famous Olympic Course in San Francisco is called "the course that was built in reverse." The reason for this is that in 1922 the Olympic Club, a private social club purchased a course near Lake Merced called Lakeside. The course was located on the bare side of a large hill that ran down to the lake. The Olympic Club began planting trees to outline each of the eighteen holes. They planted eucalyptus, pine and cypress trees that matured in about twenty-five years to become an essential part of the challenge and beauty of Olympic, as we know it today. The fact that trees were planted on an existing course rather than having holes carved out of existing woods gave birth to the expression "built in reverse."

I'm not sure who should get the credit for this statement but I remember hearing a pro talking to some spectators once and he said, "If you can afford only one lesson, tell the pro you want it to be on the fundamentals: the grip, the stance, and the alignment."

The two lowest rounds on the PGA Tour were:
59 by Al Geiberger in 1977
59 by Chip Beck in 1991

UPDATE:
As this book was being printed David Duval shot 59 in the final round of the 1999 Bob Hope Classic, to win by one stroke and became the third "Mr. 59."

Top ten in most consecutive victories on Tour.

◇ ◇ ◇

Byron Nelson 1945 --- 11

Ben Hogan 1948 --- 6

Jackie Burke Jr. 1952 --- 4

Walter Hagen 1923 --- 4

Joe Kirkwood Sr. 1924 --- 4

Bill Melhorn 1929 --- 4

Horton Smith 1929 --- 4

Gary Player 1978 --- 3

Nick Price 1993 --- 3

Tom Watson 1980 --- 3

◇ ◇ ◇

Tom Weiskopf's first check on Tour was for $487.50 which he won at the Western Open.

Remember ..... confidence is everything.

A ball of solid gutta-percha, a milky substance derived from the latex of Malayan and Indian rubber trees was fashioned in 1845 by Rev. Dr. Patterson. Although Dr. Patterson applied for the first patent for making the gutta ball there were still many historians who claim that the balls were being made prior to Dr. Patterson's claim. These new balls were unstable causing an erratic flight, which caused problems for many golfers. Later it became apparent that the smooth surface was the problem. To correct this golfers started scratching and denting the surface of the ball. They would use everything from knives to hammers and chisels. Another problem with the gutta ball is that it could break apart. That was the reason this early rule was adopted. "If a ball splits into separate pieces, another ball may be laid down where the largest portion lie."

At the 1990 Australian Open at Royal Melbourne, Bret Ogle used a 2-iron to try and hit a ball from a bunker past a tree. The ball hit the tree, bounced back and broke Ogle's kneecap.

In the United States, we are always hearing the term "Championship Course." Across the pond they do not use that term until a championship has been played on the course.

During a tournament Gene Sarazen received this note. "Don't look for me but I'll be in the gallery." The note was attached to a orange tie that he believed was from a Ziegfield showgirl. The note went on to say that the writer desperately wanted Sarazen to beat Walter Hagen at the 1922 Westchester-Biltmore tournament. Sarazen, out of natural curiosity, kept scanning the gallery for the "showgirl" who sent the letter and lost his concentration. When Hagen complemented him on his orange tie, Sarazen realized who had really sent him the tie and note.

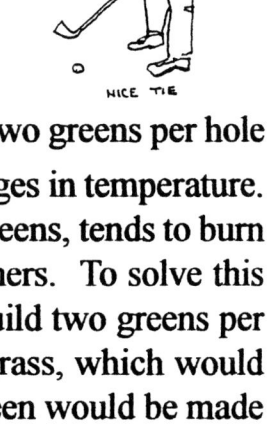

Many golf courses in Japan have two greens per hole because the climate has extreme ranges in temperature. Bent grass, the preferred grass for greens, tends to burn out quickly in the hot, humid summers. To solve this problem, the Japanese decided to build two greens per hole. One green would have bent grass, which would be regrown each year. The other green would be made with korai, a very tough grass imported from Korea which can withstand harsh winters. By doing this the Japanese clubs can offer their members two greens, one for summer and one for winter.

Never bet with someone you meet on the first tee who has a deep suntan, a 1-iron in his bag, and squinty eyes.

The year was 1985:

- Calvin Peete won the Tournament Players Championship.

- Kathryn Crosby withdraws the Crosby name from the PGA Tour event at Pebble Beach.

- Andy North won the U.S. Open.

- Curtis Strange blew a four shot lead allowing Bernhard Langer to win the Masters.

- Lanny Wadkins is the Player of the Year.

- Don Pooley won the Vardon Trophy with a 70.36 but is 46th on the money list.

- Nancy Lopez won the LPGA Championship.

- Arnold Palmer won the Senior Tournament Players Championship by 11 strokes.

- Sandy Lyle won the British Open.

- Curtis Strange won the Canadian Open.

- Roger Maltbie won the NEC World Series of Golf.

- Peter Thomson won a record 9 Senior events.

Why do we call it a "divot" to describe a piece of earth dislodged by the golf club? Simple, remember Scotland the place golf started? Divot is a Scottish word for "a piece of turf."

Bobby Jones and Jack Nicklaus have great records in the U.S. Open but with a little help from the "golf gods" their records could have been better. They both won the event four times but they also were both runner ups four times.

Gil Morgan, who is burning up the Senior Tour at the moment was never a household name on the PGA Tour. He did have some success though winning seven events. His best year on the money list was in 1978 when he was second on the list.

An Analyst is a Psychiatric specialist who treats individuals suffering from the delusion that playing golf is a form of pleasure.

The height of a flagstick should be a minimum of seven feet.

The putting surface of the fifth green at the International Golf Club in Bolton, Massachusetts is 28,000 square feet. In case you didn't know the greens of an average golf course average between eight to ten thousand square feet.

Golf bags weren't introduced until around 1870. Up until that time caddies carried the players clubs in a bundle under their arm.

Before 1764, golf courses had twenty-two holes. In 1764, the Royal and Ancient Golf Club combined eight of their holes into four bringing the total down to eighteen. After that the rest of the clubs followed.

In baseball you hit your home run over the right-field fence, the left-field fence, or the center-field fence. Nobody cares. In golf everything has to go right over second base. (Ken Harrelson)

Top ten standing in All-Time PGA Tour Victories.

◇ ◇ ◇

Sam Sneed --- 81

Jack Nicklaus --- 70

Ben Hogan --- 63

Arnold Palmer --- 60

Byron Nelson --- 52

Billy Casper --- 51

Walter Hagen --- 40

Cary Middlecoff --- 40

Gene Sarazen --- 38

Lloyd Mangrum --- 36

◇ ◇ ◇

Golf is a game in which the slowest people in the world are those in front of you, and the fastest people in the world are the one's behind you.

I'm third in earnings, and first in spending. (Tony Lema)

Lowest known round, according to a Ripley's "Believe it or Not" cartoon of 1936, was a 55 made by E. F. Staugaard on the 6,419 yard Montebello Park Golf Club, in California. Staugaard had 13 birdies, two eagles, and three pars. His score was later tied in 1962 by Homero Blancas, a University of Houston golfer. Blancas shot his 55 at the Premier Golf Course in Longview, Texas. However, the course measured only 5,002 yards.

Chi Chi Rodriguez once said "I was so poor, I grew up under a sign that said, Made in Taiwan."

There are three ways to improve your game:
Take lessons, practice constantly, or start cheating.

Reportedly this is true and must be the longest putt in history. Playing in a friendly match in which each player was limited to one club, R.W. Bridges chose a putter. He made a hole-in-one measuring 196 yards at the Woodlawn C.C., in Kirkwood, Missouri in 1931.

"There are no rich Mexicans. They get some money, they call themselves Spanish." (Lee Trevino)

I had the thrill of being a caddie at the 1984 Senior PGA Championship, in Palm Beach Florida. While I was on the practice tee with my man, a gentleman came up to Billy Casper, who was next to me and said, "your looking good." Mr. Casper looked at him and replied, "boy I hate to hear that. There's three stages in life; youngsters, middle aged, and your looking good."

There was over 259 million Titleist golf balls sold in 1997.

The USGA has funded the University of Georgia project that produced the hybrid Bermuda grasses for most golf course for over 52 years.

While everyone is trying to win the Grand Slam, Mark Brooks achieved the distinction of winning the "Greater Slam." He won the Greater Hartford, the Greater Greensboro, and the Greater Milwaukee.

"I've never had a coach in my life. When I find one that can beat me, then I'll listen." (Lee Trevino)

John Brodie had a career as a football player, an announcer, and a member of the Senior Tour. One day his wife said to him "My God, you may get to 65 without ever working a day in your life."

In a 1988 golf study the number of U.S. golfers predicted for the year 2000 was 30 million. The number of golfers as of 1997 was just short of 27 million. I think their going to be right on the money.

After winning the 1946 U.S. Open, Lloyd Mangrum was asked if he would be interested in writing a book? He said, "Are you kidding? The only big word I know is delicatessen, and I can't even spell it."

Bob Bruce was talking to some of the Super Seniors and said, "In 30 years, we're going to be in our 90's. We're going to play three-hole tournaments for $900,000 and the one who remembers his score wins."

Over 9 million pair of golf shoes were sold worldwide in 1997. I received a pair for Christmas that I returned. I wonder if I should call so they can correct the stats?

When Bobby Jones was asked how dependent he was on his caddie, he said "If I need advice from my caddie, he'd be hitting the shots and I'd be carrying the bag."

Tommy Bolt once asked his caddie what he thought he needed and the caddie said 6-iron. Bolt said, "6-iron? It's 225 yards. What in the world makes you think it's a 6-iron?" Because that's all you have left in the bag. Except for the putter, and I'm sure it ain't a putter.

Lee Trevino had his first victory as a Tour Professional when he won the 1968 U.S. Open at Oak Hill Country Club in Rochester, New York.

One golfer had a different outlook on the game when he was accused of cheating. He said, "I don't really cheat, I've been told to play golf for my health and a good score makes me feel so much better."

"I played so bad, I got a get-well card from the IRS."

(Johnny Miller, after his 1977 season.)

When Bobby Jones competed at St. Andrews in 1921, he said it was "the worst course on earth." He even quit midway through the round. In 1964, When Jack Nicklaus was ask what he thought of St. Andrews he said, "it was a cow pasture."

There was the golfer who played every Thursday and always got home around two in the afternoon. One day he rushed in the house all out of breath at 8 pm.. Met by his worried wife, he blurted out, "I left the course at the regular time, but on the way home I had to stop to help a young women change a flat tire. In gratitude she offered to buy me a drink and one thing led to another and before I knew it we had spent the entire afternoon in a motel. I'm sorry. I'll never do it again." His wife looked him in the eyes and said "Don't lie to me, you played 36 holes, didn't you?"

Calcuttas used to be a big thing at clubs. One of the biggest Calcuttas was at the 1929 U.S. Amateur at Pebble Beach, where the total pool exceeded $200,000. Most people remember it for the big upset that took place. Bobby Jones, who was the reigning U.S. Open champion was a big favorite and was auctioned off at $60,000 but he was eliminated by Johnny Goodman in the first round.

"Hitting the ball is the fun part of golf, but the fewer times you hit the ball the more fun you have. Does that make any sense?" (Lou Graham)

The knickers that golfers used to wear were called "plus fours" because in order to create the effect of pants bloused just below the knee, manufacturers added four inches to the normal length of short pants. Thus the length of the knickers was normal length plus four inches.

The first nationally televised Skins Game took place in Scottsdale, Arizona in 1983. It saw Arnold Palmer 54, -- Jack Nicklaus 43, -- Gary Player 48 -- and Tom Watson 33, go head to head. The outcome was:

Player - $170,000   Palmer - $140,000
Nicklaus - $40,000   Watson - $10,000

After it was over Player said, "Isn't this amazing Arnold, here we've been playing for more than 30 years and it's our greatest day ever." It was also amazing to Palmer. The $140,000 he won was more than he had collected for all of his Masters and British Open wins combined. Palmer, who had also never won more than $50,000 dollars in any tournament before collected $100,000 for one days skins.

Walter Hagen won the PGA Championship five times between 1921 to 1927. He declined to defend his title in 1928 and Leo Diegel won the championship

Johnny Miller was the first golf professional to be elected into the Golf Hall of Fame by a ballot vote. To achieve this a player is required to receive 75% of the vote.

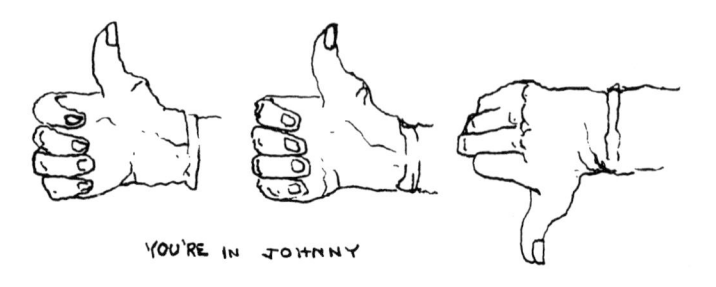

YOU'RE IN JOHNNY

Being a golfer you are going to find this hard to believe and you must be a golfer or else why would you be reading this book. Norman Manley of Saugus California, scored two consecutive holes in one in September of 1964. The hardest part to believe is that they were on back to back par four holes. One hole was 330 yards and the other was 290 yards.

Colin Montgomerie has been the leading money winner on the European Tour six consecutive years through 1998.

Here are a few of the original business cards of some well known professional golfers.

Walter Hagen

PRESIDENT

WALTER HAGEN GOLF COMPANY
901 GODFREY AVE. S.W.
GRAND RAPIDS, MICHIGAN
CHERRY 5-0451

ROBERT TYRE JONES JR.

ATTORNEY

75 POPLAR STREET N.W.
ATLANTA, GEORGIA
3-6459

Wilson®

WILSON SPORTING GOODS CO.

SAM SNEAD

ADVISORY STAFF

2233 WEST ST.
RIVER GROVE, ILL. 60171
312 456-6100

~ 41 ~

Fred Couples, obviously upset at the antics of Bill Murray at the Pebble Beach Pro-Am, said "I really like Bill, but I don't think I'd ever go down to a set where he's shooting a movie and jump and scream like a maniac."

How about Jerry Gunderson who as a kid used to roam the courses in the area where he lived in Florida looking for lost balls to sell back to golfers. As he grew older he eventually turned it into a business. At one point he was paying over $400,000 for the right to collect golf balls from over 600 courses. In one year he exported 10 million balls.

Hard to believe but supposedly true. Amateur golfer Margaret Waldron of Jacksonville Florida is legally blind and 74 years old had two holes-in-one on the same hole with the same club two days in a row. This was at Long Point Golf Course in 1990.

Jay Hebert had his first hole-in-one at the San Antonio tournament on Saturday. Then the next day he had his second hole-in-one. I got so nervous he said, "that I three putted the next two holes on both days and lost the tournament."

By the turn of the century the United States had 1,000 golf course. Ten years earlier there where only 16.

When Mike Hill decided to join the Senior Tour in 1989 he was running a little nine-hole golf course in Brooklyn, Michigan. His wife Sandy was teaching school and taking care of their three children. Between them they had about $16,000 dollars in the bank. By the end of 1991 he had topped the 2 million dollar mark in earnings.

"**S**ome of these legends have been around golf a long time....When they mention a good grip, they're talking about their dentures." (Bob Hope)

When Jimmy Demaret won the Masters in 1940 he received a check for nine hundred dollars. In 1977, just for attending the luncheon at the Masters he received a thousand dollars.

One golfer said to the other after watching a duffer digging up the course, "Should we swipe the ball for a joke?" "What joke?" said the other golfer. "The way he plays he'll never know it's gone."

Ralph Guldahl, when describing Tommy Bolt said, "Tommy Bolt threw clubs and got a mean reputation. Bob Jones threw clubs, but he became immortal."

A golfer playing in a two-ball tournament drove his tee shot to the edge of the green on a par three. His partner, playing the second shot, managed to chip it over the green into a bunker. Undaunted the first golfer recovered with a fine sand shot to within one foot of the hole. The second golfer nervously putts, and sends the ball one foot past the hole, leaving the first golfer to putt in and finish the hole. "Do you realize that we took five strokes on an easy par three?" Says the first golfer. "Yes, and don't forget who took three of them!" Answered his partner.

Golf got its name because all the other four letter words were taken.

Dumbest move in 1998 on the Senior Tour goes to Brian Barnes who forgot to replace his ball marker on the 11th hole of the final round after moving it to the side. The two stroke penalty dropped him from third to eighth.

At the 1973 Sea Pines Heritage Classic in Hilton Head, South Carolina, Hale Irwin's golf ball landed inside a woman's bra. I have no idea how this could have happened, but it did. Although the rulebook states a golfer is supposed to retrieve the ball from an obstruction and drop it, an exception was made in this case.

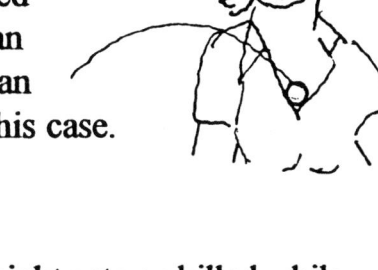

Saying things like this might get you killed while playing in a Pro-Am.
---This is more fun than the other time I played golf.
---Oops, was that your ball.
---What do you mean pick up? I can still make a 9.

When we hear the name Bob Toski we think of "golf teacher." Well Bob Toski was a fine tour player. Bob joined the tour in 1949 and gradually worked his way up the ladder to the top. He was the leading money winner in 1954. But with three small children, he decided to leave the tour at the age of 30 to spend more time with his family.

Your home course is the place where your real handicap is that everyone knows exactly what it is.

Most people play a fair game of golf.

                                        If you watch them.

On the 16th hole at Cypress Point, Henry Ransom hit a drive that hit the cliff below the green and fell to the beach below. Mr. Ransom tried three times to clear the cliff with shots. On the fourth shot, the ball bounced off the rocks and hit him in the stomach. Ransom told his caddie to retrieve the ball walked off, saying "When the hole starts hitting back at me, it's time to quit."

Bill was in the hospital being visited by his mates who asked what on earth had happened to him. He was in traction and heavily bandaged. Well Bill said, it's like this. My wife and I were playing a round of golf and we were on the 11th tee when my wife let go with a mighty hook that flew over the fence and into the adjoining pasture. After much searching I found her ball firmly jammed in a cows rear end. As I lifted the tail and discovered the ball, I jubilantly shouted out "Hey dear, this looks like yours!"

Tiger Woods was selected as the 1997 Associated Press Male Athlete of the Year and became the first golfer to receive that award in 25 years.

Golf swings are like snow flakes: There are no two exactly alike. (Peter Jacobsen)

Why did Karsten Solheim founder of Ping golf clubs, name his club line Ping? When he designed the first putter it was intended to be lightweight and feature heel-toe weighting. When Solheim tried it for the first time he was surprised to hear a rather pronounced *ping* sound when he struck the putt. Thus the "Ping" name was born. The first putter was not successful, but subsequent models made an impression on the touring pros and soon the business was off and running.

In the "When the going gets tough, the tough win" column, there's Jose Maria Olazabal. He awoke the first morning of the 1998 Dubai Desert Classic with a temperature of 102 degrees and a throat infection. His doctor recommended that he stay in bed and forget the tournament but Olazabal ignored the advice and went on to win.

Zeppo Marx once said, "The hardest shot is a mashie at ninety yards from the green where the ball has to be played against an oak tree, bounces back into the sand trap, hits a stone, bounces on the green and rolls in the hole. That shot is so difficult I have only made it once."

The Feather Ball

By 1630 the golf ball had been perfected to a leather pouch filled almost exclusively with a top hat full of down feathers from ducks or geese. The feathers were boiled to soften and shrink them prior to insertion into the leather skin that had been soaked in alum and water. The feathers were then stuffed into the leather ball. After drying out, the leather cover contracted while the feathers expanded, leaving a solid sphere with faint seams. Making the Feather ball was a tedious task and so time consuming that a days work yielded only 4 or 5 balls. The feather ball suffered from two important problems. If the ball became wet, it became very heavy and distance was greatly reduced.

Second, one topped shot with the blade of an iron and the seams of the ball could break, resulting in an explosion of feathers.

Actor Jack Lemmon is known for his acting ability and for not being a very good golfer. For years he has tried and failed to make the cut at the Bing Crosby Pro-Am. Byron Nelson once said that "Lemmon's swing looks like he is beating a chicken." Peter Jacobsen, who is Lemmon's partner at the Pro-Am said, "I've seen better swings on a condemned playground." Lemmon himself once said "I'd rather open on Broadway in Hamlet, with no rehearsals, than tee off at Pebble Beach in the tournament."

Top ten standing for most victories in a season.

◇ ◇ ◇

Byron Nelson 1945 --- 18

~

Ben Hogan 1946 --- 13

~

Sam Sneed 1950 --- 11

~

Ben Hogan 1948 --- 10

~

Paul Runyan 1933 --- 9

~

Horton Smith 1929 --- 9

~

Gene Sarazen 1930 --- 9

<>

Byron Nelson 1944 --- 8

~

Arnold Palmer 1960 --- 8

~

Johnny Miller 1974 --- 8

◇ ◇ ◇

Christmas Day is the easiest day of the year to get a tee-time at Pebble Beach.

"Most golfers prepare for disaster. A good golfer prepares for success." (Bob Toski)

After David Feherty played a Jack Nicklaus designed, course in Grand Cypress, Florida he was asked what he thought of it? He said "this place is like one of those hot-air hand dryers in toilets. It's a great idea and everybody uses it once, but never again. It takes to long."

Tony Green a member of the Scottish international team liked to take his golden retriever Ben to the links with him. One day after a practice round, Green became worried because Ben looked sick and took the dog to the vet. The vet recommended surgery to see what was causing the swelling in Ben's stomach. Well I'm sure you figured it out by now, when he opened up the canine there were eleven golf balls inside. Since then Ben has been banned from the course.

People will do anything to get into the record books. Floyd Satterlee Rood used the entire United States as a golf course. He started out from the Pacific Ocean on September 14, 1963 and with 114,737 strokes he reached the Atlantic Ocean on October 3, 1964. The course was 3,397.7 miles long and he only lost 3,511 balls.

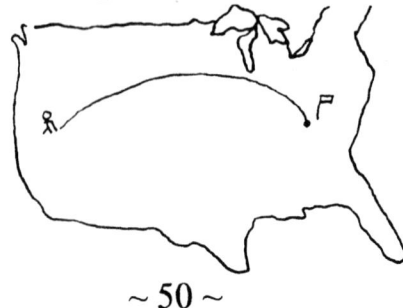

A businessman golfer is someone who talks golf at the office and talks business on the golf course.

Bob Jones was defeated in the 1929 U.S. Amateur at Pebble Beach by 21 year old Johnny Goodman who was virtually unknown to the golf world. Goodman traveled to Pebble Beach from Omaha in a cattle car. Later he went on to win the 1933 and 1937 U.S. Opens.

This story was related to me a few years ago by a man that said he was there when it happened. It seems that a group of wealthy Arab businessmen wearing their traditional headdress arrived at St. Andrews for a round of golf. When they had finished the eighteen one of them handed his elderly Scottish caddie a generous tip. The caddie said, "thanks very much, your excellency and I hope your head gets better."

The first known reference to golf in America is in 1659 when it was banned from the streets of Albany, New York.

It's not whether you win or lose,
        but whether I win or lose. (Sandy Lyle)

"I hit the ball like Doug Sanders----
        but I putted like Colonel Sanders.
                            (Chi Chi Rodriquez)

The Royal and Ancient Golf club of St. Andrews (which doesn't even own a golf course) and the U.S. Golf Association (which in made up of over 5,000 clubs) jointly make rules for the entire world of golf.

Tommy Bolt considered himself a very good dresser. In fact, nothing made him more upset than hearing about Doug Sander's sense of style. "The man looks like a jukebox with feet," he once said. "In fact, even his feet look like jukeboxes."

The main reason that Ken Venturi took up golf was that he stuttered so bad as a youngster he wanted to do something where he could be by himself.

In 1909 the USGA ruled that caddies, caddymasters and greenskeepers over the age of 16 are professional golfers. The rule was later modified and eventually in 1963 it was reversed.

The good news about golf is that great physical ability is not required to play well.

Everyone who has been around golf for awhile has heard Miller Barber referred to as "Mr. X" and assumed that it was because of the dark sunglasses he wears. Not so, my golf nut friend. It all started, as they say in the movies, back in 1961 after the Seattle Open. Miller had received a check for $10,000 for getting a hole-in-one during the tournament. As some of the golfers were getting ready to leave for the next tour stop, the Del Webb tournament in Bakersfield, Jim Ferree asked Miller to drive his car down so he could fly. They got to Bakersfield but Miller never showed up. He finally showed up about a week or so later at another tournament. He never told us where he was and still hasn't. All we know is that Miller had the car, $10,000 and a case of Canadian Club whiskey that Jimmy got in Canada for his dad. When Miller caught up to us there was only one bottle left. Hence the name ---
"The Mysterious Mr. X."

Did you know that the first national attention that Walter Hagen received was not for golf but rather for baseball. He was a minor-league baseball pitcher with great prospects and didn't turn fully to golf until he won the 1914 U.S. Open at the age of 21.

Golfer - "Do you think it's a sin for me to play golf on Sunday?" Caddie, "The way you play, sir, It's a *crime* any day of the week."

"If the pupil isn't learning, the teacher isn't teaching."

Tommy Armour's book of the 30s, "How to Play Your Best Golf All the Time" was one of the biggest selling books ever authored on golf. The book your presently reading wasn't out at the time.

Everybody knows the story about Roberto De Vicenzo signing an incorrect scorecard at the 1968 Masters but did you know that he won an astonishing 230 tournaments worldwide in his career including four on the PGA Tour and one British Open.

Did you ever play "Yardage." Instead of simply winning the hole, you win the yardage of the hole. It can be played as a two-ball, three-ball or four ball. At the end of the round the person or team with the most yardage wins. Play hard on those par fives.

"Golf is the most fun you can have without taking your clothes off." (Unknown)

Most golf balls aren't numbered high like 9, 10 or 11 anymore but in the late 50'S and early 60's, several golf ball manufacturers did number balls with double digits. Touring pros out of superstition tended to use only low numbered ball, like 1 through 3. The everyday golfer soon picked up on this practice and the manufacturers changed production accordingly.

The most important shot in golf is "the next one."

The reason that the club face on your woods is rounded from top to bottom is mostly a matter of appearance and optics. The club face is round from top to bottom to give the appearance of loft. If the face were cut straight from top to bottom, it would appear almost vertical to the golfer. By rounding, or creating "roll" golf manufacturers are actually helping golfer's confidence in getting the ball into the air.

"Golf is 20% talent and 80% management." (Ben Hogan)

<u>13 Original Rules</u>

The original 13 rules of golf were drawn up by the "Company of Gentlemen Golfers" in 1744 under the title "Articles and Laws in Playing at Golf".

The following 13 rules are phrased and spelled as they were at the time of their writing.

1. You must tee your ball, within a clubs length of the hole.

2. Your tee must be upon the ground.

3. You are not to change the ball which you stroke off the tee.

4. You are not to remove stones, bones or any break club, for the sake of playing your ball. Except upon the fair green and that only within a clubs length of your ball.

5. If your ball come among watter or any wattery filth, you are at liberty to take out your ball and bring it behind the hazard and teeing it, you may play it with any club and allow your adversary a stroke, for so getting out your ball.

6. If your balls be found anywhere touching one another, you are to lift the first ball till you play the last.

(Rules continued from page 56)

7. At holling, you are to play your ball honestly for the hole and not to play upon your adversary's ball now lying in your way of the hole.

8. If you should lose your ball, by it's being taken up or any other way, you are to go back to the spot where you struck last and drop another ball and allow your adversary a stroke for the misfortune.

9. No man at holling his ball is to be allowed to mark his way to the hole with his club or anything else.

10. If a ball is stopped by any person, horse, dog, or anything else the ball as stopped must be played where it lies.

11. If you draw you club in order to strike and proceed so far in the stroke as to be bringing down your club. If then, your club shall break in any way it is to be accounted as a stroke.

12. He whose ball lies furthest from the hole is obliged to play first.

13. Niether French ditch or dyke made for the preservation of the links nor the scholar's holes or the soldier's lines shall be accounted a hazard. But the ball is to be taken out teed and played with any iron club.

"Titleist has offered me a big contract not to play its balls." (Bob Hope)

There's an old story about Harry Vardon who won a record six British Opens. In the 1920 U.S. Open at Inverness Country Club in Toledo he missed a three foot putt on the 72nd hole and dropped to second behind Ted Ray. One of the members asked Vardon how a player of his skills could manage to miss such a short putt. This didn't set well with a player who had just lost the U.S. Open so he made the man a bet. Vardon bet the man $100 that one week from that day the member couldn't make the identical putt that Vardon had missed. Vardon also told the man that he could practice the putt all week. The man jumped at the bet. The news about the bet made all of the papers and a huge crowd showed up for the show. The member missed the putt. Vardon collected the $100 and the man got a lesson in putting under tournament pressure.

The Los Angeles Open which was started in 1926 is the third oldest surviving PGA Tour event. It also was the first tournament event to offer a $10,000 purse.

The PGA Championship and the U.S. Open were discontinued during the First World War.

Determining the good golfer from the average golfer is not always determined on the tee but more often when they don't hit the green in regulation.

The use of molds to dimple the gutta-percha balls was first started in 1880.

The term "Bogey" was invented by Hugh Rotherham, as the score of a hypothetical golfer playing perfect golf on every hole. Over the years and with the invention of the rubber-cored golf ball golfers were able to reach the greens more easily and so bogey has come to represent a one over par score for the hole.

In 1901 Sunningdale the first course to be built amidst a cleared forest, opened for play. It was the first course with grass grown completely from seed. Until then, most courses were laid out by simple routing them through meadows.

Willie Anderson was the winner of the first United States Open which was held in 1895.

Dave Hill was never one to hold back his thoughts. At the 1970 U.S. Open at Hazeltine, he was asked what he thought of the Robert Trent Jones layout. These are just a few of the things he said about the course.

<>

"It looks like a man destroyed a beautiful farm."

<>

"What it lacks is 80 acres of corn and a few cows."

<>

"Just because you cut the grass and put up flags doesn't mean you have a golf course."

<>

"The man who designed this course had the blueprints upside down."

<>

"Either of my little boys could build a better course."

The good news is that when Phil Mickelson won the 1998 Mercedes Championship he not only won the first prize of $306,000 but the keys to a new Mercedes. The bad news, if you can call it that, was he had just purchased the same model two weeks earlier.

"I'm a good player, not a great player. And good is not bad." (Fred Couples)

I'm not trying to tell you what to spend your practice time on but remember this old saying. "You can recover from a bad drive, but there is no recovery from a bad putt."

It's surprising how easy a twenty foot putt is when it's for a 10.

"**G**olf is not and never has been a fair game."
                                              (Jack Nicklaus)

Counting on your opponent to tell you when he breaks a rule is like expecting him to make fun of his own haircut.

Showing up at a golf course as an adult with your own clubs is like showing up for your final exams. It's assumed you know something about the subject.

A ball will always come to rest halfway down a hill unless there is water at the bottom.

My son Timmy reminds me of Magellan when he's playing golf. <u>He's all over the world.</u>

When you embark on a swing change, it's important to know that you will face two chief challenges ---- habit and comfort.

In 1906 Goodrich introduced a golf ball with a rubber core that was filled with compressed air. The ball which was called the "pneumatic," was very lively as you can imagine and presented a problem. In warm weather it could explode and that wasn't very good, especially if you had the ball in your pocket at the time. Due to this unsolvable problem, the ball was discontinued.

Tom Watson and Peter Thomson are the only two people with five victories at the British Open.

"**I** don't even like golf, really. I just like watching the show because I get to see places I've never been." This comment was over heard in a bar, when two men were talking about Shell's Wonderful World of Golf.

Only four men have ever won all of the four Major Championships the Masters, the U.S. Open, the British Open and the PGA Championship. They are; Gene Sarazen who was the first to do it, followed by Ben Hogan, Gary Player, and Jack Nicklaus.

The PGA Magazine was first published in 1920. At that time it was known as the Professional Golfer of America magazine. It is the oldest continually published magazine in the United States.

Who do you think became the first corporation to sponsor a golf tournament? My favorite company, The Hershey Chocolate Company sponsored the Hershey Open in 1933.

The reigning Masters and British Open champion Seve Ballesteros was the favorite to win the 1980 U.S. Open but one thing kept him from the title. A Watch. He managed to show up about seven minutes late for his tee time and was disqualified.

Only practice counts as practice.

Masters Champions at a Glance.

◇ ◇ ◇

Year	Winner	Score
1934	Horton Smith	284
1935	Gene Sarazen	282
1936	Horton Smith	285
1937	Byron Nelson	283
1938	Henry Picard	285
1939	Ralph Guldahl	279
1940	Jimmy Demaret	280
1941	Craig Wood	280
1942	Byron Nelson	280
1943	*No Tournament*	
1944	*Because of War*	
1945	*No Tournament*	
1946	Herman Keiser	282
1947	Jimmy Demaret	281
1948	Claude Harmon	279
1949	Sam Sneed	282
1950	Jimmy Demaret	283
1951	Ben Hogan	280
1952	Sam Sneed	286
1953	Ben Hogan	274
1954	Sam Sneed	289
1955	Cary Middlecoff	279
1956	Jack Burke Jr.	289
1957	Doug Ford	282
1958	Arnold Palmer	284
1959	Art Wall Jr.	284

Year	Player	Score
1960	Arnold Palmer	282
1961	Gary Player	280
1962	Arnold Palmer	280
1963	Jack Nicklaus	286
1964	Arnold Palmer	276
1965	Jack Nicklaus	271
1966	Jack Nicklaus	288
1967	Gay Brewer Jr.	280
1968	Bob Goalby	277
1969	George Archer	281
1970	Billy Casper	279
1971	Charles Coody	279
1972	Jack Nicklaus	286
1973	Tommy Aaron	283
1974	Gary Player	278
1975	Jack Nicklaus	276
1976	Ray Floyd	271
1977	Tom Watson	276
1978	Gary Player	277
1979	Fuzzy Zoeller	280
1980	Seve Ballesteros	275
1981	Tom Watson	280
1982	Craig Stadler	284
1983	Seve Ballesteros	280
1984	Ben Crenshaw	277
1985	Bernhard Langer	282
1986	Jack Nicklaus	279
1987	Larry Mize	285
1988	Sandy Lyle	281

Masters Cont.

Year	Player	Score
1989	Nick Faldo	283
1990	Nick Faldo	278
1991	Ian Woosnam	277
1992	Fred Couples	275
1993	Bernhard Langer	277
1994	Jose M. Olazabal	279
1995	Ben Crenshaw	274
1996	Nick Faldo	276
1997	Tiger Woods	270
1998	Mark O'Meara	279

You know your getting older when your friends stop asking you about the condition of your game, and start asking you about the condition of your health.

It's just my opinion but twenty-five million people saw Roberto de Vicenzo birdie the 17th hole at the 1968 Masters. I think that would hold up in court.

What does your group call it when you are "closest to the pin" on a par three? We call it a "greenie" but in various other parts of the country it is called a "gink, skin, sweets, or barrellhead.

The pros of the past would turn over in their graves if they saw the amount of money that can be won on tour now. Years ago you were the top money winner if you won five or ten thousand dollars. In 1998 the top money winners on each of the three tours totaled 6.5 million between them.

        Hale Irwin - - - 2.8 million (Senior Tour)
        David Duval - - - 2.5 million (PGA Tour)
        Annika Sorenstam - - - 1.2 million (LPGA Tour)

A friend of mine related this story to me and I'll let you be the judge. Nick and his friend were playing one day when they heard the old cry "Fore". They both immediately jumped behind a short, bushy tree. They no sooner got behind the tree when they heard the ball crash into the branches. They lifted their heads to look for the ball but couldn't find it anywhere. The golfer who hit the ball joined them and after a few minutes they gave up the search and hit their shots to the green. When they got to the green, Nick's friend reached into his pocket for his "putting ball" you know how that is, and he pulled out two balls, his putting ball and the Top/Flite 2 the ball the other golfer had hit into the tree. When Nick asked him how it got there he said he had no idea. He said it must have just bounced in his pocket off of the tree without him noticing it. I know what your thinking but this gentleman has been a priest of over forty years.

When Byron Nelson was on his hot streak in 1945, he set an all time PGA Tour record of 11 wins in a row and a record of 19 consecutive rounds under 70. His earnings for his eleven straight wins was $30,000. I imagine that was good at that time but that eleven win total was less than 30th place money in the 1999 Mercedes Championship.

In 1942 the United States government halted the manufacturing of golf equipment for the duration of the war.

Sometimes it doesn't pay to get out of bed as Tommy Nakajima found out during the 1978 Masters. On the par 5, 13th hole Tommy gambled on his drive but put it into the creek on the left. He took a drop and a one stroke penalty then laid up short of the green. This approach hit and then backed up into the water in the front of the green, but the ball was playable. He tried to hit this shot on to the green but failed to clear the hazard and the ball rolled back and hit his foot. Two more penalty strokes. Then to put the icing on the cake, his caddie dropped a club in the hazard for two additional strokes. The moral of this story is, "Don't try to do something your not at least 90% sure you can do and don't hire a caddie who's all thumbs."

Golf was televised for the first time in 1947, on a local St. Louis telecast of the U.S. Open.

When Bob Rosburg was in his prime he never consulted a yardage book, he played by sight. In one tournament he was paired with a player that consulted his yardage book for every shot. On one hole the player hit the ball over the green. On the next hole he left the shot short. The more the player checked the yardage book the worst he played and the slower he got. Finally Rosburg had seen enough. He said, "Boy, if you didn't have that yardage book you'd be in a hell of a mess."

The USGA Golf Journal was founded in 1948.

The USGA and the R&A completed a newly revised Rules of Golf in 1951. Some of the big changes to come out of the conference were the legalization of the center shafted putter worldwide. The out-of-bounds penalty is standardized at stroke-and-distance and the stymie is finally and forever abolished.

The graphite golf shaft was invented in 1973.

Why we yell "fore".

A major change took place in Scotland in the last decade of the 18th century. At that time the play was different than it is now. Rather than taking turns striking the ball all of the golfers would stand by their tees and they would all take their swing at the same time. If there happened to be anyone walking on the course in the direction of their swing, they would all shout "four" in unison, to warn the walker that there had been four swings taken and four balls were aloft. Of course, in the rare occurrence that the players were a pair, they would naturally shout "two" or whatever number corresponded to the number of balls struck. "Four" became a common word heard on the golf course and associated with golf. It elicited an immediate response as it represented a warning. Then the rules were changed for reasons lost in history. Each golfer took his swing in turn, rather than all at once. And yet, the need for a warning to others walking in the path of the ball was still present. Since the most common warning had always been "Four" it remained so. Over time, since it no longer represented the number four, the spelling changed to "Fore."

Will Rogers once said "golf has made more liars out of people than the income tax."

"A pretty girl will always have the toughest time learning to play golf, because every man wants to give her lessons." (Harvey Penick)

In 1954 the Wilson Sporting Goods Company asked Gene Sarazen to go to the U.S. Amateur and take a look at a kid from Pennsylvania called Palmer. After it was over and Palmer had won the U.S. Amateur Sarazen called Wilson to tell them that he won but that he didn't think he would ever amount to a hill of beans. Sarazen said, "He made a lot of putts but he was all over the lot."

Davis Love found himself paired with Lee Trevino in the PGA Championship. Love liked to keep to himself and block out any distractions in order to play well. He figured the best thing to do was to just tell Lee right up front so that there would be no problem. "Lee," he said, as they were leaving the first tee, "I'm pretty nervous, so if it's all the same to you, I don't think I'll do much talking." "That's okay, Davis," said Trevino. "All you have to do is listen. I'll do enough talking for both of us."

The PGA National opened in Palm Beach, Florida in 1964.

Dumbest move on the LPGA goes to Wendy Ward at the 1998 Office Depot Tournament when she accepted a ride from the 18th green to the first tee at the turn of the second round. The two stroke penalty still left her with a two shot lead but she eventually finished tied for third.

If you want to improve your golf game, you have to except long periods when your efforts can seem wasted, when your scores don't reflect the effort your putting in. These will be the times when patience and perseverance will be the most important traits you can have.

(Dr. Bob Rotella)

The old days at the U.S. Open wasn't as strict as they are today but they still had rules to follow as Porky Oliver was to find out. It seems that at the 1940 U.S. Open old Porky, Johnny Bulla, Dutch Harrison, Ky Laffoon, Duke Gibson, and Claude Harmon were finishing lunch when they noticed storm clouds rolling in. They wanted to get ahead of the storm so they divided up into two threesomes, headed for the course and teed off twenty-eight minutes ahead of their starting times. This resulted in their disqualification and was costly for all off them but especially painful for Porky Oliver. He shot 71 in that final round which made his total 287 and would have tied him with the champion, Lawson Little.

Golf Digest was founded in 1951 with Bill Davis as the editor.

"**N**ow here's Jack Lemmon, about to play his all important eight shot." That was how Jim McKay reported the play at Pebble Beach's 14th hole during the 1959 Crosby.

Ben Hogan was once asked what advice he would give struggling young players. "Watch out for buses," Hogan said.

"**T**wo of my favorite celebrities are comedian Bing Crosby and singer Bob Hope. Or is it the other way around? I always forget which one thinks he's funny and which one thinks he can sing." (Jimmy Demaret)

A chip shot is a short, low approach shot that gets you into position for one or more missed putts.

Roberto DeVicenzo won the first U.S. Senior Open in 1980.

Doug Sanders once said, "I'm working as hard as I can to get my life and my money to run out at the same time. If I can just die after lunch Tuesday, everything will be perfect."

In 1963, Arnold Palmer became the first professional to earn over $100,000 in official prize money on the PGA Tour in one year.

Doug Weaver, Mark Wiebe, Jerry Pate and Nick Price all had aces on the par-3, sixth hole the same day in the U.S. Open at Oak Hill in 1989.

Do you remember the long putt that Nick Faldo made on the second hole at Augusta? It was 100 feet and the longest putt made to date at the Masters. Faldo went on to win the tournament.

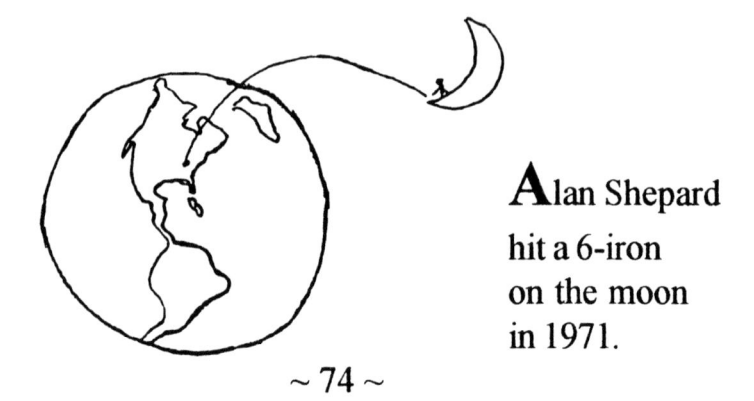

Alan Shepard hit a 6-iron on the moon in 1971.

Another, in the thousands of Tommy Bolt stories. It was 1960 and the U.S. Open was at Cherry Hills Country Club in Denver. Bolt was having a frustrating round when he came to the 18th hole and snap hooked two drives into a pond. He walk to the front of the tee, looked at the driver and sailed it into the pond. There was a young boy in the crowd who immediately dove in the pond and came up with Bolt's driver. Bolt took out his money clip and started over to the boy to show his appreciation but never got the chance. The boy took off through the gallery, over the fence and gone.

Golf Magazine was founded in 1959, with Charles Price as the first editor.

"People are always wondering who's better, Hogan or Nicklaus. Well, I've seen Jack Nicklaus watch Ben practice, but I've never seen Ben watch anybody else practice. What's that tell you?" (Tommy Bolt)

Harvey Penick's Little Red Book became the all-time best selling golf book in 1991.

The Mid-Amateur started in 1981.

I'm not trying to suggest that Sam Sneed is a little tight with his money but I have heard rumors that Sam still has two dollars of the first dollar he ever made. One time after a bad first round and feeling a little tired Sam was thinking about dropping out because his chances of making the cut were somewhere between slim and none. Just as he was about to make a decision he overheard someone say that all those who play 36 holes, regardless of the score or cut, would get a minimum of $1,000. Sam didn't make the cut but he played 36 holes.

Patty Berg and "Babe" Zahaias were the first women elected to the World Golf Hall of Fame.

During the 1934 U.S. Open at Merion, Bobby Cruickshank was very much in contention. After a good drive into the valley he had to carry a brook in front of the green with his approach shot. He hit the shot a little "fat" and the ball plopped into the water. To everyone's amazement, it hit a rock in the brook and bounced on to the green. Cruickshank was so elated that he threw his club into the air and turned to the gallery in disbelief. As everyone cheered, the club came down and hit him squarely on the top of the head knocking him to his knees. "Aye," said Bobby, "that's the first time I've made par hitting two rocks on the same hole."

The pay of a first-class caddie going 18 holes at St. Andrews in 1875 was 1.5 shillings. I have no idea what 1.5 shillings is equal to in U.S. currency. So your asking yourself, why did he put this fact in if he didn't know if it was equal to 20 cents or 20 dollars? Maybe just to give you something to do.

"Through years of experience I have found that air offers less resistance than dirt." (Jack Nichlaus)

The fee charged by golf architect Rees Jones to remodel the Black Course at Bethpage State Park, in preparation for the 2002 U.S. Open: <u>Free</u> - No charge.

Tommy Bolt is famous for his temper tantrums and for throwing a club now and then. In 1957, the day after the PGA adopted the "Tommy Bolt Rule", prohibiting the throwing of clubs, Bolt threw a club just because he wanted to be certain he would be the first golfer fined under the rule.

The definition of a chronic cheater in golf is a person who gets a hole in one and puts zero on the scorecard.

When Jack Nicklaus was in his prime, Johnny Miller said. "When Jack Nicklaus plays well, he wins. When he plays badly, he finishes second. When he plays terribly, he finishes third."

The National Hole-in-One Clearing House was established by *Golf Digest* in 1952.

We have all heard the statement that women have a good short game. Well at the 1982 Lady Michelob Classic in Atlanta, Joan Joyce proved it. On her way to a final round of 67, she completed the 18 holes with only 17 putts. Three - two putt greens, eleven - one putt greens and four times she holed out from off the green.

A good golfer makes 200 decisions a round. You can't make good decisions when your angry.

The man was obviously having problems repeating the oath in the witness box. The judge looked down contemptuously, "Do you know how to swear?", he asked, "Of course I do, your honor," came the reply, "I'm a caddie."

The first one million dollar purse on the PGA Tour was at the Panasonic Las Vegas Invitational in 1986.

"Golf is the only game in which a precise knowledge of the rules can earn one a reputation for bad sportsmanship." (Patrick Campbell)

"Hitting the golf ball and putting have nothing in common. They have two different swings. You work all of your life trying to perfect a repetitive swing and then you get to the green and you have to do something that is totally unrelated. There shouldn't be any cups, just flagsticks. The person who hits the most fairways and greens and got closest to the flagstick would be the tournament winner." (Ben Hogan)

In 1969 Nancy Lopez won the New Mexico Women's Amateur by beating 23 year old Mary Bryan, 10 and 8 in the final. The real news here is that Nancy Lopez was 12 years old at the time.

The youngest person to win the PGA Championship was Gene Sarazen, in 1922 at the age of 20.

Golfer - I never played this badly before!
Caddie - I didn't realize you had played before!

In 1969 at the Michigan Classic the PGA Tour had to come up with the money when the tournament officials welshed on the purse.

When John McDermott won the United States Open in 1911 he set the record for the youngest winner at the age of 19.

Thirteen years after the PGA Tour dropped the "Caucasian only" clause from it's bylaws, Lee Elder became the first black golfer to gain an invitation to the Masters by defeating Peter Oosterhuis in a playoff at the 1974 Monsanto Open.

When Curtis Strange won the U.S. Open at Oak Hill he became the first player to win back-to-back U.S. Opens since Ben Hogan did it in 1950-51. The bad news is that Curtis Strange hasn't won on the PGA Tour since then.

"The fairways were so narrow you had to walk down them single file." (Sam Snead)

Before there were real caddies at the Augusta National, golfers would recruit bellhops from the Bon Air Hotel. This is where most of the out of town members stayed.

Only 22% of all golfers regularly score better than 90. Only 6% of all golfers regularly score better than 80.

Ben Hogan, Sam Snead and Byron Nelson are all born in the same year, 1912.

Sam Snead played in his first U.S. Open in 1937. Leading by one stroke after three rounds Snead shot 71 in the finally round but was overtaken by the charging Ralph Guldahl, who shot 69. That was the closest Snead would ever get to winning the U.S. Open, the one major that he never won.

In 1954 Ed Furgol won the first <u>nationally</u> televised golf Tournament, the U.S. Open at Baltusrol.

Walter Hagen said, "If you three putt the first green, they'll never remember it. But if you three putt the 18th they'll never forget it."

Beth Daniel, JoAnne Carner, Sally Little and Patty Sheehan won ten Mazda cars plus a lot of cash between them in 1982 as part of the Mazda LPGA Series. What's the old aphorism. "Drive for show but putt for dough." I think in this case they must have been doing both well.

A school teacher was talking her first golf lesson.
"Is the word spelled p-u-t or p-u-t-t," she asked the instructor. "P-u-t-t is correct," he replied. "Put means to place something where you want it. Putt means merely a vain attempt to do the same thing."

"**V**ictory is everything.... You can spend money but you can never spend the memories." (Ken Venturi)

When Tom Watson was asked why he didn't pursue a high school baseball career, he said "I could only hit balls thrown at my feet."

You are going to find this extremely hard to believe but I seen a book at the library titled "How to control your temper on the golf course." The hard part is that it was by Tommy Bolt.

Wood is the type of golf club a golfer uses to drive the ball a long distance. Woods is where a golfers ball usually lands after it has been driven a long distance.

Rookie Lanny Wadkins won his first PGA Tour event at the 1972 Sahara Invitational, in Las Vegas. Wadkins had an outstanding rookie year and finished 10th on the money list. 1972 was also the rookie year for Tom Watson.

Do you remember the heartbreak of T.C. Chen in the 1985 U.S. Open? After gaining a first round lead which was help by a double eagle on the 2nd hole, he came to the last day, with a four shot advantage. On the 5th hole he double hit a chip shot out of the heavy ruff and took a quadruple bogey. It cost him the four shot lead and he eventually lost the tournament by one shot.

There are over 16,000 golf courses in the U.S.A..

The year was 1958 and.....

Ken Venturi won three tour events in six weeks.

Arnold Palmer jumps into the national spotlight when he won his first Masters with a 4-under par 284.

It was kind of appropriate that Gary Player, a person who loves horses would win his first tournament on Tour at the Kentucky Derby Open, in 1958.

Mickey Wright claims her first major title the LPGA championship at Churchhill Valley C.C. in Penn Hills, Pennsylvania.

Tommy Bolt won the U.S. Open at Southern Hills Country Club in Tulsa by four strokes after leading in after every round. This was his only win in a major.

For the first time the PGA Tour players tee off in the PGA Championship under a "stroke play" format. One reason for this was that stroke play was more suited for television.

1958 Continued

Bob Rosburg with a scoring average of 70.11 is chosen as the winner of the PGA Tour's Vardon Trophy.

Tour veteran, Horton Smith is inducted into the PGA Hall of Fame. Horton Smith had eight victories in 1929 and won the Masters twice in his career.

Dow Finsterwald won the PGA Championship by overtaking the third round leader Sam Snead and finishing two strokes better than Billy Casper.

Patty Berg won the last of her record 15 majors when she won the Western Open.

Australian Peter Thomsom won the British Open and became the ninth golfer to win the tournament four times. This also made him only the second man to win four times in five years. Young Tom Morris was the other man.

"**I** never pray to God to help me make a putt. I pray to God to help me react good if I miss a putt."

(Chi Chi Rodriquez)

At the 1960 U.S. Open, Jack Nicklaus who was then an amateur, beat all of the pros except for Arnold Palmer to finish with the silver medal. This was the best showing of an amateur since 1933 when Johnny Goodman won the U.S. Open.

Have you ever played in a flag tournament? In this type of tournament each player is given a small flag to carry with him. He has to stick the flag in the ground at the exact spot where his ball lies after he has taken the number of strokes equal to par plus his handicap. For example, a 12 handicapper playing on a course where par is 72 would place the flag where his ball lies after he has hit his 84th shot. Whoever carries his flag the farthest around the course wins the tournament.

One note: To avoid having six or seven people making it all the way to the clubhouse with their flags, I have found it better to give everyone only 50-75% of their handicap strokes. That way only someone who has a better then average round will still have their flag when they reach the clubhouse.

"Forget the PGA Tour, there's no money in it."
Titanic Thompson, giving advice to Lee Trevino in 1966.

In 1992, it was a Fred Couples year. He won a million dollars by Spring. He won the Masters. He led the PGA Tour money list with $1,344,188. He was named PGA Player of the Year and won the Vardon Trophy.

This might make you feel good, bad, inadequate, or it might even make you want to practice. On January 28, 1995 a gentleman named Cy Young of Delray Beach, Florida made two holes-in-one at the Par-3 Lakeview Golf Course. What makes this so amazing is that Mr. Young is 70 years old and only has one arm. The first hole, 96 yards he hit a 3-iron right in the hole. Then on number 13, a 107 yard hole he used a 3-wood.

Doug Sanders had twenty career Tour victories. Five of them were in 1961. He was also runner up three times that year. One of the second place finishes was at the Masters. That would be as close as he would get to winning a major in his career.

Golf should only by played on days ending in y.

"You have to make corrections in your game a little bit at a time. It's like taking your medicine. A few aspirin will probably cure what ails you, but the whole bottle at once might just kill you." (Harvey Penick)

Harry Vardon played his last round of championship golf while trying to qualify for the 1932 British Open, which he had won six times. He failed to make the cut.

Hubert Green won the 1977 U. S. Open despite receiving a death threat before the final round.

In 1933 Gene Sarazen urged the PGA to go to an eight inch diameter cup saying that the game "needs greater thrills." The eight inch cup was tried in the Gasparilla Open in Tampa, Florida January 1933 but that was about as far as it went.

George S. May who was the promoter of the World and All American Championships, disclosed that in 1951 he paid Ben Hogan $15,000 to play in the event. Hogan refused to play in the event in 1952 without the same guarantee.

1981 Do you remember ?

Arnold Palmer comes from six shots behind to win the U.S. Senior Open.

Bill Rogers wins the British Open and is named Player of the Year.

Neon colored balls hit the proshop shelves.

A 23 year old rising star, Berhard Langer led the European money list and was second in the British Open.

Nicklaus says good-bye to his long time caddie Angelo.

Donna Caponi records five victories for the second year in a row.

Tom Kite was the top money winner.

The ultimate example of indecision was when Arnold Palmer brought eight putters to the Colonial at Fort Worth.

"Call me a clown, call me a nice guy, but don't ever call me collect." (Chi Chi Rodriquez)

Vice President Spiro Agnew, hit his playing partner Doug Sanders on the head with a stray shot on the first hole of the 1970 Bob Hope Desert Classic pro-am.

Think back to 1991. In the Doral Ryder Open, Paul Azinger got disqualified when a TV viewer calls the tournament after noticing Azinger move loose impediments in a hazard. I don't know how you feel about this but has anyone ever watched a play in baseball, football, basketball (need I go on) and called in and had the ruling changed? Where do these people get these phone numbers anyway and how did he get through to "the powers to be"?

"I don't play for the scores; I like to play fast."

(George Bush)

Arnold Palmer had eight victories in 1960, which is the most since Sam Snead had eleven in 1950. Arnold's victories earned him just over $75,000 and the title of top money winner that year but the Vardon trophy went to Billy Casper with a scoring average of 69.95.

"Until you play it, St. Andrews looks like the kind of real estate you couldn't give away." (Sam Snead)

Irving Hemmle of Fort Worth, Texas hit 48,265 range balls in 1983. That's the way my luck goes. I owned a driving range from 1983 to 1992 in St. Louis, Missouri. See what I'm getting at? I'm in St. Louis and he's in Fort Worth. He could have made my first year getting started in business a lot easier if he just would have moved.

Ken Venturi nearly won the Masters Tournament as an amateur in 1956 when he fired opening rounds of 66-69-75 to take a four shot lead into the last day. On Sunday he had six bogeys on the back nine to shoot 80 and watch Jackie Burke pass him and get the green jacket. "This was a bitter disappointment," Venturi said. "I hope and pray some day I'll be able to wear one of those green jackets." Unfortunately, he never would.

"Golf is like solitaire. When you cheat you only cheat yourself." (Tony Lema)

Dr. Joseph Boydstone of Bakersfield, California had three holes-in-one recorded in the same round. Granted they were on a par-3 course but still he gets a "wow" from me.

March of 1938 the Federal Trade Commission ordered eight manufacturers and the PGA of America to stop price fixing on golf balls.

Balata verses Surlyn covered golf balls. We all know golfers that have a 18 or 20 handicap and insist on using only Titleist balatas because of the better "feel." Here's a shocker for them. It has been conclusively proven that when balls with no identifying marks were given to a group of test golfers to hit, none could tell the difference between the Surlyn and the Balata.
The main difference in the Balata ball is that it will spin more, giving an exceptional player the ability to shape shots. For the average golfer a Balata ball will just turn your fade into a slice and the draw (if by some miracle you ever hit one) into a sweeping hook.

What happened in 1969?

◇ ◇ ◇

George Archer hit his 2nd shot into the water on the par-5, 15th at Augusta National, but he managed to save par and won the Masters by one shot over Billy Casper, Tom Weiskopf and George Knudson.

Kathy Whitworth ties Mickey Wright's LPGA record for the most consecutive wins in a year by winning four times.

Former Army sergeant Orville Moody became the dark horse winner at the U.S. Open when he defeated Deane Beman, Al Geiberger and Bob Rosburg by one shot at the Champions G.C. in Houston, Texas.

Donna Caponi won the U.S. Women's Open at Scenic Hills C.C. in Pensacola, Florida. Her final round of 69 was enough to ensure her first Tour victory.

Hollis Stacy, age 15, becomes the youngest winner of the U.S. Girls Junior Championship with her win at Brookhaven C.C. in Dallas, Texas

1969 Continued

Gary Player won the Tournament of Champions by two shots over Lee Trevino.

Tony Jacklin became the first Englishman in 18 years to win the British Open with his victory at Royal Lytham.

Raymond Floyd won the PGA for his first win of a major championship, even though his Sunday round was a shaky 74.

Orville Moody won the World Series of Golf held for the winners of the four major championships.

Dave Hill won his first Vardon Trophy.

Orville Moody was named PGA Tour Player of the Year.

Kathy Whitworth won her fourth career Vare Trophy.

In 1936 the R&A was so concerned that the golf ball was becoming too lively they asked the golf ball manufacturers to produce a "slower" ball. It seems as if they had a distance problem back then just like we do now and they didn't have titanium, graphite, or large club heads.

Have you ever played horseshoes on the putting green? Well, before you grab the stakes and the shoes, let me explain. "Horseshoes" is a great game for the putting green. Two or more players can play but two is ideal. The game is played just like horseshoes. Each player gets two putts at the hole. The putts should be a minimum of 15 feet. The scoring would go like this:
> 3 points for a made putt. (Same as a ringer in horseshoes.)
> 1 point for closest to the hole. (Again like horseshoes.)
> If neither player makes the putt but player A's two putts are closer to the cup than either one of player B's putts, player A gets two points.
> If neither makes the putt, but player A has the closest ball and player B the second closest ball, player A gets one point.
> The player who scored points on the two putts has the honor to go first on the next series of two putts. Play continues until one player reaches 21 points.

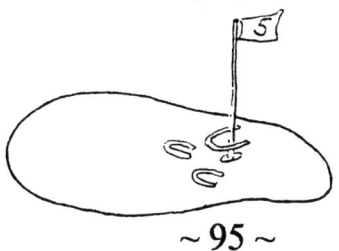

"No power on earth will deter men from using a ball that will add to the length of his drives."
(Golf Illustrated - 1902)

Billy Casper won the 1970 Masters Tournament by beating Gene Ltittler 69-74, in an 18-hole playoff.

Overheard at a Senior Tour event: "What's nice about the Senior tour is that you can't remember the bad shots."

Since 1986 the number of golfers in the United States has increased by 35%.

"No one would ever again win that much money in a single year on the tour." That is what most of the pros were saying in 1938 when Sam Snead won eight PGA Tour events and $19,000.

John Byron Nelson won his first professional tournament in 1935 at the New Jersy State Open.

What happened in 1984?

◇ ◇ ◇

Tom Watson became the PGA Player of the Year for a record 6th time.

Jack Nicklaus claimed his 70th victory by winning at the Memorial Tournament.

Corey Pavin wins Rookie of the Year.

Tom Kite, Gary Koch and Peter Jacobsen were double winners for the first time in their careers.

Ben Crenshaw won the Masters Tournament, Fuzzy Zoeller won the U.S. Open and Lee Trevino took the PGA Championship.

After a long dry spell Hubert Green, Larry Nelson and Bill Kratzert discovered the old magic and each picked up a victory late in the year.

The "stymie" wasn't outlawed by the R&A and the USGA until 1951.

A few years ago, actually now that I think about it, it was about 12 years ago I was asked to play at a very prestigious club in my area. Well it didn't take me thirty seconds to say yes. In fact if I remember right, I said yes before I knew the day and time. While we were on the putting green before our tee time, one of the gentlemen I had just met asked if I wanted to get in their "low ball, ten cents a hole" game? I told him he could count me in. I was thinking the membership at the club was $40,000 and here we were going to play for dimes. Well about ten minutes before we were do to tee off, I overheard two players in our group talking about me. A little later one of the gentleman came over and apologetically asked if I would mind dropping out of the ten cents a hole game. He explained that a few of the group, of which there was eight, felt uneasy because I didn't have a registered handicap. I told him, "no problem, I was just happy to play the course." As the round progressed I realized how lucky I was. Not because I was playing a course that I had always dreamed of playing but because I hadn't been allowed in the game. You see, the one thing that I didn't realize, was that the bet doubled each hole and they were playing carry-overs. The "pay off chart" on the next page will show you why I felt so lucky.

~ 98 ~

Payoff chart

Hole	Payoff	Hole	Payoff
1	$.10	10	51.20
2	.20	11	102.40
3	.40	12	204.80
4	.80	13	409.60
5	1.60	14	819.20
6	3.20	15	1,638.40
7	6.40	16	3,276.80
8	12.80	17	6,553.60
9	25.60	18	$13,107.20

Doubling after each hole with carry-overs, hole number 18 could have gotten pretty expensive.

Record books wouldn't lie would they? Well this one is in the record books but I'll let you be the judge. The longest drive ever hit in competition was 515 yards by 64 year old, Mike Austin at the National Seniors Open in 1974. It was at the Winterwood Golf Club in Las Vegas and he had help from a 35 m.p.h. tail-wind. His tee shot actually went 65 yards past the green on a 450-yard par four.

The first time President Dwight D. Eisenhower broke 90 was at Augusta National G.C. when he shot 88 on April 20, 1953 and beat Senator Robert Taft.

Highlights and Lowlights of 1971

◇ ◇ ◇

When Jack Nicklaus won the PGA Championship this year, he became the first to win all four majors twice.

Lee Trevino became the first person to win the national titles of Britain, United States and Canada in one year. The U.S. Open and the Canadian Open were won in playoffs and the British Open was won by one stroke. The other amazing thing about this string of major wins is that it all took place in a span of only 21 days. With play like that, it's no wonder that the Associated Press named Lee Trevino Athlete of the Year for 1971.

Arnold Palmer pocketed $250,000 when he won the Tour's richest event, the Westchester Classic in New York.

Johnny Miller won the first PGA Tour title of his career when he won the Southern Open Invitational.

(1971 Continued)

Laura Baugh won the 1971 U.S. Women's Amateur, becoming the youngest winner on record at age 16. Two years later she joined the LPGA Tour but never won a tournament in her 20 year career as a pro.

Bobby Jones Jr. died at the age of 69 after a long battle with a crippling spinal ailment that gradually paralyzed his arms and legs.

Kathy Whitworth led the LPGA in earnings, was named player of the year and won the Vare Trophy.

Jack Nicklaus and Lee Trevino both had five PGA Tour wins but Nicklaus led earnings with $244,490.

JoAnne Carner won her first U.S. Women's Open title by beating Kathy Whitworth by seven shots.

Arnold Palmer and Jack Nicklaus successfully defend the National Team title.

They say that Walter Hagen was the first man to make a million dollars in golf and spend it. Sam Sneed was the first to make a million and save two.

After Tommy Bolt had finished a poor round with a caddie he thought was particularly incompetent, he motioned to a tour official that he needed a ruling. When the official came over he said, "I know you can get fined for throwing a club. What I want to know is if I can get fined for throwing a caddie?"

The inaugural Doral Open was held on March 25, 1962 and was played on the Blue Course at Doral C.C. in Miami, Florida.

Larry Nelson had an easy 4-shot victory in the 1981 PGA Championship thanks to a pair of 66's in the two middle rounds.

The 1980 Master Tournament was an easy runaway for Seve Ballesteros. Leading by 10 shots with nine holes to play, he was able to stumble a little and still record a four shot victory over Gibby Gilbert and Jack Newton.

Why do many pros insist that their caddies carry the extra balls in their pockets?
This practice is known as "warming the eggs." Many pros believe that warming the golf balls help them to fly farther. While warming does help the elasticity of the ball, it would require illegal means to raise the temperature of the ball enough to get any significant benefits from it.

The first metal wood was introduced by Taylor Made in 1979.

The first sand wedge was invented and introduced by Gene Sarazen in 1932.

Why are pin placement made as they are in tournaments? There are no specific rules in regard to the location of pins. However, at most PGA events the holes are usually cut six on the left, six on the right and six in the middle of the green so as not to favor players who prefer to draw or fade the ball. Greenskeepers also try to keep the ground flat around the cup and consider the type of shot required to get the ball close.

Just because your fifty years old it doesn't mean you can't get hot. Isao Aoki carded a 60 at the Emerald Coast Classic to set a Senior Tour low-round record.

The Bridges, a new course designed by Arnold Palmer in Bay St. Louis Mississippi, has over 4,000 feet of bridges.

Did you know that it wasn't until the advent of the steel shafted clubs in the 1920's that manufacturers began building matched sets of clubs? This is also the time that the practice of numbering the individual clubs became popular. Prior to this the wooden shafted clubs were sold individually.

Contrary to popular belief Tiger Woods did not lead the tour in driving distance in 1997. John Daly did, averaging 302 yards. Tiger Woods average was 294.8 yards.

Betsy Rawls won the 1957 U.S. Women's Open after the apparent champion Jackie Pung was disqualified for signing an incorrect score card.

While in college at the University of Houston, Fred Couples roomed with Jim Nantz, a commentator now for CBS.

Everyone remembers that Larry Mize pitched in from 140 feet to win a sudden death playoff with Greg Norman in the 1987 Masters. Did you remember that Seve Ballesteros was in that playoff and was eliminated earlier?

One day I overheard one golfer ask another golfer. "I'd be interested to know what your handicap is these days." "I'm a scratch golfer. I write down all my good scores, and scratch out all of my bad ones."

About 90% of all Senior PGA Tour players use ceramic unipole magnets for pain relief and increased circulation.

A sand trap is a deep depression filled with sand filled with golfers in a deep depression.

When Hubert Green was asked the difference between him shooting 81 on the first day of the U.S. Open and 67 on the second day, he said "fourteen strokes."

In 1979 the PGA Tour adopted the "one-ball rule." This meant that a player must play the same brand and type of ball for the entire round. The rule stopped the practice of switching from a two-piece ball to a wound ball to gain an advantage on some shots.

One day at the Masters, Byron Nelson was talking to O.B. Keeler, an Atlanta newspaper man who had written stories about Byron Nelson from time to time. Keeler had a great love for poetry and told Byron that the way he played today reminded him of a poem by Lord Byron. Reporters who were gathered around overheard the remark and the next day all the papers referred to Byron Nelson as 'Lord Byron'. The name stuck from that day on.

Although Tom Weiskopf never won a U.S. Open he did set some records. In 1972 at Peeble Beach he scored 4-3-2-1 for the four rounds that he played the short par-3 7th hole. In 1978 at Cherry Hills he became the first golfer to make two holes-in-one in the same tournament.

Remember 1983 ?

◇ ◇ ◇

Isao Aoki holed out a wedge shot from 128 yards on the last hole of the Hawaiian Open to take the victory away from Jack Renner. It was one of those typical golf holes. Aoki pushed his drive, then snap hooked a fairway wood into the rough and then holed the wedge.

Dumbest mistake of the year. Make that the century. Hale Irwin whiffed a two-inch putt at the British Open and finished the event one stroke behind Tom Watson.

Jay Sigel became the first golfer since Bobby Jones to win two USGA championships in the same year. He won the U.S. Amateur and the Mid-Amateur.

Kathy Whitworth won her 84th Tour Event tying Sam Snead's record.

Raymond Floyd won the Vardon Trophy without a single victory and only one second place finish.

Golf is not a game of great shots. It's a game of the most accurate misses. (Gene Littler)

The word "Tee" probably comes from the Scottish *teay*, a small pile of sand. For many years golfers would make a pile of sand or dirt and place their ball on top of it for driving.

During the turn of the century, Coburn Haskell with the help of the Goodrich Tire & Rubber Company created the rubber core ball constructed by winding many yards of "strip" rubber around a marble-size central core. This was then covered with a skin of gutta-percha. One fault of the new ball was the effect on the golf courses. Holes had to be lengthened and numerous hazards had to be moved further out to catch the shots that missed the fairways. The ball was slow to catch on until Alex Herd used it while winning the Brittish Open.

A man was cured of deafness when a golf ball hit him in the head. He was thrilled and told his friends, "That's two things I was cured of in one day." What's the other, asked his friend? "Hanging around golf courses," he replied.

"**G**olf is a better game played downhill."

(Jack Nicklaus)

Chris Perry played in 377 PGA Tour events before he recorded his first victory at the B.C. Open. Brad Bryant and David Ogrin went longer than that before they got their first win.

When Byron Nelson had his streak of 11 wins he was paid one of the highest compliments an American athlete can receive. His picture was put on boxes of Wheaties. For this honor he was paid $200.00.

"**T**he difference between a sand bunker and water is the difference between a car crash and a airplane crash. You have a chance of recovering from a car crash."

(Bobby Jones)

It takes a lot of guts to play this game, and by looking at Billy Casper's shape lately, you can tell he certainly has a lot of guts.

Sam Snead became the assistant pro at the Greenbier in White Sulphur Springs, West Virginia when he was 23 years old. He almost lost his new job when his drive on the 335 yard fifth hole reached the green and hit the rear of Alva Bradley, president of the C&O railroad, which owned the hotel at that time. Bradley thought that Snead had hit into them while they were still on the green. The next day Bradley ask Snead to play with his group and he again drove the 5th green. When they got to the 16th tee, Bradley pointed to a fairway bunker 270 yards away and asked Snead, "Can you drive into that?" "No," said Snead. "If I try to bunt my drives, it ruins my game." Snead then hit his drive 75 yards passed the trap.

"If you're going to be in the limelight, you may as well dress for it." That is what Jimmy Demaret said after wearing a canary yellow shirt and matching slacks at the 1947 Master, which he won.

Jack Nicklaus, after winning the 1986 Masters at the age of 46 said, "I'm not as good as I was 15 years ago. Just occasionally, I want to be as I once was and I was that today."

"A perfectly straight shot with a big club is a fluke."

(Jack Nicklaus)

The United States Golf Association was formed in 1884 and it didn't take long for their first ruling. In the first U.S. Amateur, when Richard Peters decided that he was going to putt with a billiard cue, they banned it.

The old conceded putt, or was it? Bill Campbell, the great American amateur learned a valuable lesson the hard way in the finals of the 1952 Canadian Open. Campbell and his opponent had been giving each other short putts throughout the match. Playing the 34th hole of the 36-hole final, Campbell stood 2-up. Both players were faced with three foot putts. Campbells putt was for a par and the Championship, his opponents was for bogey. His opponent made his putt and walked off to the next tee. Campbells putt hung on the lip and he raked it back to try again, thinking he had halved the hole. When he reached the next tee, his opponent asked if he made the putt. "No you saw me miss it," said Campbell. "No, I meant the little one," said the opponent. "I didn't give it to you." Instead of being 2-up with two to play, Campbell was just 1-up. When his opponent birdied the next hole, the match was even and went into sudden death. Campbell lost on the first playoff hole.

Did you know that Greg Norman is allergic to grass?

The cost to construct a golf course today is in the millions of dollars. The cost to construct the original six hole golf course in 1892 at The Country Club in Brookline, Massachusetts, was fifty dollars.

Why do we call sand traps bunkers?
Story has it that bunkers came from the Scottish word *bonker*, meaning a chest or box were coal is kept, usually dug into the side of a hill. Often cows would graze in the marshlands adjacent to the old links courses, standing along the dunes and creating a depression that reminded Scottish players of these chest, and eventually these areas became known as bunkers.

Lee Trevino was the first person to make one million dollars on the senior tour in one year.

"One of the advantages bowling has over golf is that you seldom lose a bowling ball." (Don Carter)

Playing in the 1991 Tradition, a Senior PGA Tour event, Jack Nicklaus found himself trailing by twelve shots after the first two rounds. In true Nicklaus fashion he shot 66 and 67 in the last two rounds to win the tournament. One of the writers covering the tournament asked Frank Beard, if Nicklaus was really that good. "No," said Beard. "He's just been on a thirty-year lucky streak."

Gary Player was preparing to tee off in the 1965 U.S. Open at Bellerive C.C. in St. Louis, when he noticed the large scoreboard that had all the past champion's names. Ken Venturi's (the defending champion) name was in gold. Player said that he actually saw his name in gold next to Venturi's. "I took it as an omen," said Player, and he went on to win the championship.

Do you remember Scott Hoch losing the Masters when he missed a two foot putt in the first hole of the sudden death playoff. That sent the playoff to the second hole where Nick Faldo won the Championship.

One afternoon Lee Trevino was cutting the grass in the front yard of his Dallas home. A woman was driving by and rolled down the window. She asked him how much he was getting paid to do the yard work. "Nothing," he said. "The lady of the house lets me sleep with her." The women drove off in a hurry.

Early in his career, Lanny Wadkins played some friendly matches with Ben Hogan. About half way through one of these rounds, Hogan was called to the clubhouse and had to quit, with Lanny ahead. A few days later Lanny received a check from Hogan for fifteen dollars. Several weeks later Lanny received a call from Hogan's secretary asking if he had cashed the check. "No, and you can tell Mister Hogan not to worry about it," he said. "I'm never going to cash it, I may even frame it."

Leo Diegel used to offer a rather unique bet to local amateurs. He would offer to play them a match in which he would hit his shots on the front nine standing on just his right leg. On the back nine he would switch and stand on the left leg. If they seemed like they wanted a chance to get their money back (he rarely lost the bet) he would offer to play one more nine and he would hit his shots standing cross-legged.

C ary Middlecoff was one of the most deliberate players of all time. He would make Bernhard Langer look like a fast player. During one of "Shell's Wonderful World of Golf" matches he'd fidget and waggle, move around, change clubs, and start all over until he felt comfortable and ready to hit the shot. This meant that they had to do a lot of cutting on the film to get the show to fit in. When Middlecoff saw the film of his match he said, "There, did you see that? My pre-shot routine was way too fast. I was out of my rhythm."

N ot that I want to keep harping on poor old DeVicenzo signing an incorrect score card and losing the Masters. BUT-- You do know that the person you are pared with keeps your score in tour events, don't you? Well did you know who put that wrong score on the card? If you said Tommy Aaron, you know your golf.

T he 1963 U.S. Open was held at The Country Club in Brookline, Massachusetts. When Tony Lema came to the difficult par-3 16th hole he tried to determine what club to hit. He look at the tops of the trees near the green. He also tried to check the wind by looking at the flag. He finally grabbed a few blades of grass and dropped them from his fingers. The grass blew straight back up into the air. That's when Tony Lema realized this was no ordinary golf course.

Babe Ruth loved to play golf. One time on a trip to Bermuda he was invited to play at the Mid-Ocean Club. This was a wonderfully designed course by C.B. MacDonald. When he came to the 5th hole, a 370 yard par-4 he asked the caddie for his driver. The caddie suggested that he should lay up and take the lake out of play. "Give me the driver," Babe said. "I could throw it on the green from here." After fifteen balls went to a watery grave, Ruth broke the driver over his knee and walked in to the clubhouse.

Jimmy Demaret was playing in the Bing Crosby National Pro-Am one year. When he got up and looked out the window on Sunday morning he saw Pebble Beach covered with snow. "I know I got drunk last night, but how did I wind up at Squaw Valley?" He asked.

When Dale Douglass was asked, "How long it took him to prepare for the Senior Tour," his answer was simple, "Fifty Years."

If you have an interesting golf story about the Tour or about yourself or a great golf joke send it to us.
If we use it in the next book we'll send you a free copy.
Our address is on the following page.

For more information on this book or one of our other books listed below, please contact us at:

◇ ◇ ◇ ◇

Evad Enterprises
P.O. Box 463
O'Fallon, MO 63366

◇ ◇ ◇ ◇

The F Book
Fun - Facts - Figures
and other "F" words
Famous - First - Fabulous

~~~~

Fun, Facts & Figures
Volume Two
A book of Tid-Bit & Trivia

~~~~